"There is an old proverb that says 'Thoughts disentangle themselves when passing over the lips and through the finger tips.' The 17:18 Series, which encourages us to actually write out the words of Scripture, will be a tremendous tool in putting that proverb into action in our daily lives. I am happy to commend this project."

–Jerry Bridges, a longtime staff member of the Navigators and author of *The Pursuit of Holiness*

"Several years ago I read an article about copying the Scriptures hand. I tried it with the Pastoral Epistles, writing out all three bo with a fountain pen in my journal, and found it a profitable exerc I am glad to see this series of journals appear, and I hope they widely used."

–Donald S. Whitney, Associate Professor of Biblical Spirituality, Southern Baptist Theological Seminary, Louisville

The 17:18 Series

The Book of Revelation

Joel R. Beeke and Rob Wynalda

This book belongs to:

_____

Given by: _____

Date: _____

Revelation
© 2015 by Full Quiver LLC
www.fullquiver5.com

Published by
Reformation Heritage Books
2965 Leonard St., NE
Grand Rapids, MI 49525
616-977-0889 / Fax 616-285-3246
e-mail: orders@heritagebooks.org
website: www.heritagebooks.org

ISBN 978-1-60178-389-9

Cover Design: Bethany Sanderson and Steve Coy
Journible® Design: Rob Wynalda

Why the 17:18 series?

In Deuteronomy 17, Moses is leaving final instructions concerning the future of Israel. As a prophet of God, Moses foretells of when Israel will place a king over the nation (v. 14). In verses 16 & 17, he lists items that the king could not do as king. In verse 18, he transitions to what he should do as king.

The king is commanded not to simply acquire a copy of the law (the entire book of Deuteronomy) from the "scroll publishing house," but to handwrite his own copy of the law. The purpose of such a copy written by his own hand was so that:
* he would read it
* he would learn to fear the Lord
* he would obey the commands of God
* his heart would not become proud
* he would not turn to the right or the left from following the law (Prov. 4:27)
* also, his sons would serve in the kingdom after him (Deut. 17:19, 20).

Thirty-four hundred years later, educators are "discovering" that students who physically write out their notes by hand have a much greater retention rate than those who simply hear or visually read the information. Apparently, God knew this to be true for the kings of Israel also.

From such understanding came the conception of this series of books.

Have a great time writing and learning the Word of God,

Rob Wynalda
Romans 1:16

The Purpose of the Journible®

Engagement:

The Journible® is a profoundly simple attempt to aid a person's ability to engage the Word of God by slowing down the process of simply reading the text. The book is organized so that the "scribe" can slowly and thoughtfully engage the text while leaving plenty of room to write comments and questions about the text (Deuteronomy 17:18; Psalm 119; 2 Timothy 3:16, 17).

Legacy:

Journibles® provide a legacy to pass on from one generation to the next. The Journible® creates an opportunity for one generation to communicate in writing to the next generation their insights and personal applications of the text (Deuteronomy 6).

How to use this book

This book is organized so that the scribe (you) will handwrite your very own copy of Revelation. You will be writing the text of the Bible only on the right-hand page of the book. This should make for easier writing and also allows ample space on the left page of your open text to write your own notes and comments. From time to time a question or word will be lightly printed on the left page; these questions are to aid in further study, but should not interfere with your own notes and comments. This means that you are encouraged not only to write your own "copy" of the Bible, but also to write your own notes concerning the text.

Yes, we are setting aside our mass-produced Gutenberg Bibles and attempting to get back to the simple handwritten copy of the text.

Notes

Revelation

Revelation is prophecy, calling God's people to stay faithful under persecution in hope of Christ's coming. It is apocalyptic, a depiction of the battle between good and evil in vivid symbols. It is an epistle, a personal letter written to seven churches in the Roman Empire. How should each of these aspects of Revelation affect how we read the book?

Notes

(1) What is the full title of this book? What does that mean?

(3) Who is blessed by God?
(See also 14:13; 16:15; 19:9; 20:6; 22:7, 14.)

(4–5) Who gives grace and peace?

Revelation 1:1-6

1

2

3

4

5

6

Notes

(8) What does this verse reveal about God?

(9) Why was John on Patmos?

Revelation 1:7-11

7

8

9

10

11

Notes

(13) Compare this to Daniel 7:9, 13—14. What does this communicate about Christ?

(17) What does it mean that Christ is "the first and the last"? (See v. 8.)

Revelation 1:12-18

12
13
14
15
16
17
18

Notes

(20) What do the seven lampstands (or candlesticks) represent?

Revelation 1:19-20

19

20

Notes

(1) What was Ephesus' religious history?
(See Acts 18:19–19:41; 20:17; 1 Tim. 1:3.)

(2) How could Ephesus test a person's claim to be an apostle?

(4) What was their "first love"? (Compare with v. 19.)

(5) What does it mean to repent?

Revelation 2:1-6

1
2
3
4
5
6

Notes

(7) Explain the call to "hear." Where else is this found in Scripture?

(9) How can poor and persecuted Christians be "rich"?

(11) Explain the "second death." (See 20:6, 14; 21:8.)

Revelation 2:7-12

7
8
9
10
11
12

Notes

(13) Who was Antipas, and what happened to him?

Revelation 2:13-17

13

14

15

16

17

Notes

(19) How can it encourage Christians that Christ knows our works?

(20) Why is this woman called "Jezebel"? (See 1 Kings 16:31; 2 Kings 9:22.)

(22) What is one purpose of suffering?

Revelation 2:18-23

18

19

20

21

22

23

Notes

(27) How does Christ apply Psalm 2:9 to faithful Christians?

(28) What is the "morning star"? (See 22:16; Num. 24:17.)

Revelation 2:24-29

24
25
26
27
28
29

Notes

(1) What was wrong with Sardis?

(3) How is Christ's coming like a thief?

(4) When and why would one be dressed in white? (See Eccl. 9:7–8; Dan. 7:9.)

Revelation 3:1-6

1.

2.

3.

4.

5.

6.

Notes

(7) What does the key of David symbolize? (See Isa. 22:22; Matt. 16:19.)

Revelation 3:7-11

7

8

9

10

11

Notes

(12) What does it mean to be a "pillar" in God's temple?

(14-16) Unlike nearby cities, Laodicea had neither hot springs for bathing nor cold water for drinking, but only lukewarm water via miles of aqueducts. How did Christ use this to communicate His view of this church?

(17) How could they have all these problems and yet not know it?

Revelation 3:12-17

12

13

14

15

16

17

Notes

(20) What does eating with them symbolize?

(22) What does it mean to have ears that hear?
(See Deut. 29:4; Isa. 6:9–10.)

Revelation 3:18-22

18

19

20

21

22

Notes

(2) Why is God depicted as sitting on a "throne"?

(3) What does a rainbow symbolize? (See Gen. 9:12–17.)

(5) How is the Holy Spirit's work like the shining of lamps?

Revelation 4:1-6

1
2
3
4
5
6

Notes

(8–11) What can we learn about worship from this scene?

Revelation 4:7-11

7
8
9
10
11

Notes

(1) The scroll represents God's will or plan. Why would it be sealed?

(4) Why was John weeping?

(5-6) How is Christ like a lion? Like a lamb?

Revelation 5:1-6

1

2

3

4

5

6

Notes

(9—10) Why is the Lamb able to open the scroll?

(12—13) How can the angels worship God and the Lamb?

Revelation 5:7-12

7

8

9

10

11

12

Notes

Revelation 5:13-14

13

14

Notes

(1) What does the Lamb's opening each seal teach us about Him?

(2) Who is the rider on a white horse? (See 19:11; Ps. 45:4–5.)

(3–6) How do the second and third seals match Christ's predictions? (Matt. 24:7)

Revelation 6:1-6

1

2

3

4

5

6

Notes

(9—11) What does this imply about what will happen to the church?

Revelation 6:7-11

7

8

9

10

11

Notes

(15-16) What is it that makes all men equal?

(17) Answer their question: Who can stand?

Revelation 6:12-17

12

13

14

15

16

17

Notes

(4) What is the symbolism of 144,000 (12 × 12 × 10 × 10 × 10)?

(5) Why is Judah first? (See 5:5.)

Revelation 7:1-6

1

2

3

4

5

6

Notes

(9) What does this reveal concerning the kingdom of God?

(11–12) What should salvation produce?

Revelation 7:7-12

7

8

9

10

11

12

Notes

(14) What is the "great tribulation"?

(15) What will it mean for God to dwell with His people?

(17) What is "living water"? Where else is it mentioned in Scripture?

Revelation 7:13-17

13

14

15

16

17

Notes

(1) Why is heaven silent? (See Ps. 46:10; Zech. 2:13.)

(3) How are the prayers of believers like "incense"?

(6–12) Compare these trumpet judgments with the plagues of Exodus 7–12.

Revelation 8:1-6

1
2
3
4
5
6

Notes

Revelation 8:7-11

7
8
9
10
11

Notes

Revelation 8:12-13

12

13

Notes

(4) Who are those sealed by God? (See 7:3.)

(5) What do the locust-scorpions represent? (See Luke 10:17–19.)

Revelation 9:1-6

1.
2.
3.
4.
5.
6.

Notes

(11) Who is the angel of the pit or abyss?

Revelation 9:7-13

7

8

9

10

11

12

13

Notes

(15–16) In what sense do fallen angels love war and cause it?

Revelation 9:14-19

14

15

16

17

18

19

… Notes

(20-21) What does this reveal about the hearts of men?

Revelation 9:20-21

20

21

Notes

(1) Whom does this angel resemble? (See 1:16; 4:3.)

(3) Whose coming is alluded to in the roaring of a lion? (See 5:5; Isa. 31:4.)

(4) Why does God remind us that some things are sealed and not written down?

Revelation 10:1-6

1
2
3
4
5
6

Notes

(9) Why is the scroll sweet and yet bitter? (See Ezek. 3:3, 14.)

Revelation 10:7-11

7

8

9

10

11

Notes

(1) What is the new covenant temple? (See 1 Cor. 3:16.)

(3) How many years are in forty-two months? How many days?

(4) What do candlesticks (or lampstands) represent? (See 1:20.)

(5) What might the fire represent? (See Jer. 5:14; 20:9; 23:29.)

Revelation 11:1-6

1
2
3
4
5
6

Notes

(8) What do Sodom and Egypt have in common?

(11-12) What is the hope of the persecuted church?

Revelation 11:7-12

7

8

9

10

11

12

Notes

(15) What does the seventh trumpet bring?

(18) How can the dead be judged?

Revelation 11:13-18

13

14

15

16

17

18

Notes

(19) In whom is the ark of the covenant fulfilled? Why does it appear here?

Revelation 11:19

19

Notes

(1) Who is the woman? (See v. 17; Gen. 37:9–10; Song 6:10.)

(5) Who is her child, and why was He taken to God? (See Ps. 2:9.)

Revelation 12:1-6

1

2

3

4

5

6

Notes

(9) When is Satan cast down? (See Luke 10:18; John 12:31; 16:11.)

(10) What does it mean for Satan to be the accuser? (See Job 1:6–11.)

(11) How does one overcome Satan?

Revelation 12:7-11

7

8

9

10

11

Notes

(15) What might the flood or river symbolize? (See Ps. 18:3-4, 16.)

(16) What does it mean that the earth swallowed it up? (See Ex. 15:12.)

(17) Who are the offspring of the woman?

Revelation 12:12-17

12

13

14

15

16

17

Notes

(1–2) What powers does the beast represent? (See Dan. 7:3–6, 17.)

(4) Why do men worship the beast?

Revelation 13:1-5

1

2

3

4

5

Notes

(7) Who are the saints? (See 14:12.)

(8) How can Christ have saved His people from before creation? (See Eph. 1:4; 2 Tim. 1:9.)

(11) What does it mean that this beast looks like a lamb but talks like a dragon?

Revelation 13:6-11

6

7

8

9

10

11

Notes

(15) Roman emperors expected to be worshiped. How does this happen in modern nations?

(16) How is the mark of the beast a symbol of the opposite of the seal of God? (See 7:3—4; 9:4.)

Revelation 13:12-16

12

13

14

15

16

Notes

(18) What might the number 666 mean in light of Revelation's frequent use of the number 7?

Revelation 13:17-18

17

18

Notes

(1) Where have we read of the 144,000 before?

(4) How does being spiritual "virgins" contrast them with Babylon? (See v. 8; 17:1–2.)

Revelation 14:1-5

1
2
3
4
5

Notes

(6–7) How does this angel represent the mission of the church?

(8) What is Babylon, and how is it fallen?

(10–11) What will happen to those who worship the idols of this world?

Revelation 14:6-10

6

7

8

9

10

Notes

(13) What two blessings are promised to those who die in the Lord?

Revelation 14:11-16

11

12

13

14

15

16

Notes

(20) How did an ancient winepress work, and how is it an image of God's judgment?

Revelation 14:17-20

17

18

19

20

Notes

(1) How is God's wrath finished when Revelation is not done?

(3–4) What attributes of God do His judgments reveal?

Revelation 15:1-5

1

2

3

4

5

Notes

(6) Whom do the angels resemble in their golden girdles or sashes? (See 1:13.)

(8) Why was the temple filled with smoke? (See 1 Kings 8:10–12.)

Revelation 15:6-8

6
7
8

Notes

(2) Compare the first bowl/vial to the sixth plague on Egypt (Ex. 9:8—10).

(3—4) Compare the second and third bowls/vials to the second and third trumpets (8:8—11) and the first plague on Egypt (Ex. 7:17—18).

Revelation 16:1-7

1

2

3

4

5

6

7

Notes

(9) How do the wicked respond to God's judgments? Why?

(10) Compare the fifth bowl/vial to the fifth trumpet (9:1—5) and ninth plague on Egypt (Ex. 10:21—23).

(12) Compare the sixth bowl/vial to the sixth trumpet (9:13—16).

Revelation 16:8-13

8
9
10
11
12
13

Notes

(15) How must we prepare for Christ's coming at an unexpected time?

(17–21) Compare the seventh bowl/vial to the seventh trumpet (11:15–19).

Revelation 16:14-19

14

15

16

17

18

19

Notes

(21) Why would men blaspheme God?

Revelation 16:20-21

20

21

Notes

(1–2) How is worshiping false gods like prostitution? (See Deut. 31:16.)

(3) What is the "scarlet beast"? (See 13:1.)

(5) Explain her title.

Revelation 17:1-6

1
2
3
4
5
6

Notes

(9) Rome was built on seven hills and ruled a great empire (v. 18). How was that city an example of worldly and wicked power?

Revelation 17:7-11

7

8

9

10

11

Notes

(14) Why will Christ overcome the wicked?
Why will Christ's people overcome?

(17) Who controls the wicked powers of this world? For what purpose?

Revelation 17:12-17

12

13

14

15

16

17

Notes

Revelation 17:18

18

Notes

(1) What does the brightening of the earth communicate? (See Ezek. 43:2.)

(4) Why must believers separate themselves from the world? How must they do so?

Revelation 18:1-6

1
2
3
4
5
6

Notes

(7) What does the heart of the harlot Babylon reveal?

(8) What is the point of "in one day"?

(10) How is this world like the "great city Babylon"? (See Isa. 21:9; Jer. 51:1—9, 45.)

(12—13) How does this list reflect what the world loves most?

Revelation 18:7-12

7
8
9
10
11
12

Notes

(15–19) Why would merchants and sailors grieve its destruction?

Revelation 18:13-18

13

14

15

16

17

18

Notes

Revelation 18:19-22

19

20

21

22

Notes

(23–24) For what crimes will God destroy Babylon?

Revelation 18:23-24

23

24

Notes

(1-2) Why is it right to praise God for judging the wicked?

(4) What does "Amen" mean? What does "Alleluia" or "Hallelujah" mean?

Revelation 19:1-6

1

2

3

4

5

6

Notes

(7) What is the wedding of the Lamb? Who is the bride?

(10) What does the angel's response teach us about worship?

(11-16) Summarize what this vision shows about Christ.

Revelation 19:7-12

7

8

9

10

11

12

Notes

(17) How does the calling of the birds illustrate how many people will be destroyed when Christ returns? (See Ezek. 39:17–20.)

Revelation 19:13-18

13

14

15

16

17

18

Notes

(20) What is the fate of political and religious leaders who oppose Christ?

Revelation 19:19-21

19

20

21

Notes

(2) When was Satan defeated and bound? (See 12:9; Matt. 12:28–29; Col. 2:15.)

(4–6) How can these promises encourage persecuted Christians?

Revelation 20:1-5

1

2

3

4

5

Notes

(8) How many people follow Satan in the end? What does this show about mankind?

Revelation 20:6-10

6

7

8

9

10

Notes

(12) Why does God here judge men by their works? (See Matt 7:17-23; Eph. 2:8-10.)

(14) Why is the lake of fire called the second death?

Revelation 20:11-15

11

12

13

14

15

Notes

(1) Why will there be a new heaven and new earth? (See Gen. 3:17; Rom. 8:21.)

(2) How can a city be a bride?

(3) What is the essence of heaven?

(6) What is the water of life? (See Jer. 2:13; John 4:14.)

Revelation 21:1-6

1

2

3

4

5

6

Notes

(8) What action does this list of sins call us to take?

(12–14) What do the names on the city reveal about who lives in the new creation?

Revelation 21:7-12

7.

8.

9.

10.

11.

12.

Notes

(18—21) What do the building materials show about the beauty and wealth there?

Revelation 21:13-19

13

14

15

16

17

18

19

Notes

(22–23) Why do the people need no temple or sun?

(26) How will the nations contribute to the new creation?

Revelation 21:20-27

20

21

22

23

24

25

26

27

Notes

(1) What does the symbolism of water flowing from the throne mean?

(2–3) Why is the new creation compared to the garden of Eden (Gen. 2)?

(4) How can we see God if He is an infinite spirit?

(6) Why is it important that we know these promises are faithful and true?

Revelation 22:1-7

1
2
3
4
5
6
7

Notes

(12—13) Who is speaking here? What does that teach us about Him?

Revelation 22:8-14

8

9

10

11

12

13

14

Notes

(15) Why can unrepentant sinners not enter the city of God?

(16) How is Christ the "bright morning star"?

(18–19) Why is it such a great sin to add to or subtract from God's Word? (See Prov. 30:5–6.)

(20–21) How do these two verses summarize the hope and confidence of all true Christians?

Revelation 22:15-21

15

16

17

18

19

20

21

Notes

Notes

Notes

Notes